## Copyright © 2021
## by Khadizhat Witt

All rights reserved. No part of this publication may be reproduced, distributed, or transmitted in any form or by any means, including photocopying, recording, or other electronic or mechanical methods without the prior written permission of the author, except in the case of brief quotations embodied in critical reviews and certain other noncommercial uses permitted by copyright law. For permission requests, contact the author at the email below.

## circumwanderers@gmail.com

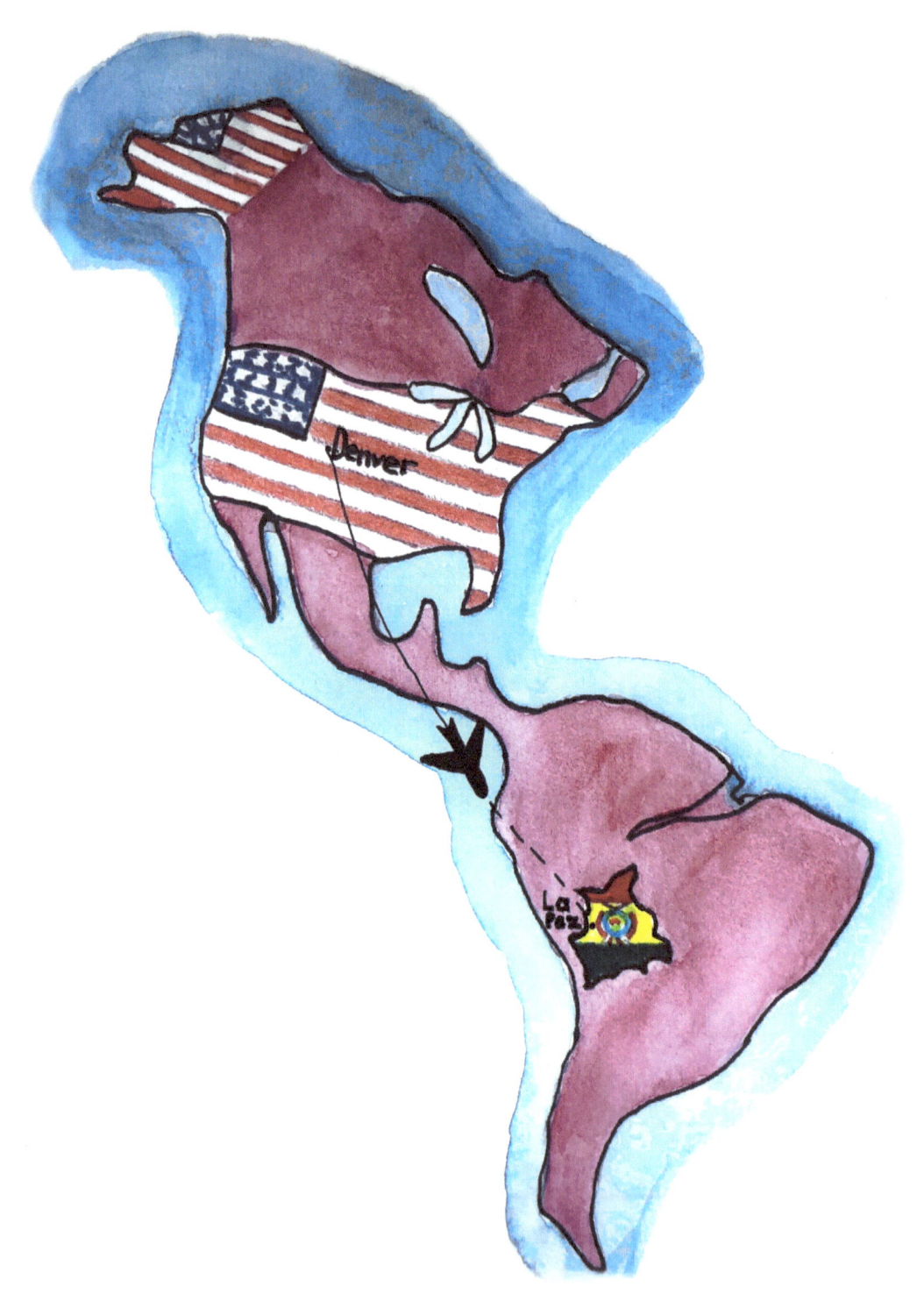

School break is around the corner and the adventurous family is preparing for a journey to South America. This time George, Kate and their kids, Aya and Nick are going to explore Bolivia.

A big part of Bolivia's territory is at a very high elevation. The family spends a few days in Colorado, USA, where they get used to high altitude. From Denver they fly to La Paz, Bolivia's administrative capital.

La Paz is situated 3,640 meters (12,000 feet) above sea level. Upon landing they feel the difference in air pressure and notice the vibrant life of the Bolivian city.

The kids immediately spot cable cars rising above them.

"Is there a ski resort here?" wonders Aya.

"Not exactly," answers George. "This cable car system is called TELEFÉRICO. It connects the area of El Alto, where we landed at the airport, with La Paz, where we will stay for a couple of days. It is an efficient system of public transport, like a metro line. Would you like to ride in it tomorrow?"

"Yessss!" shout kids at the same time.

In the morning, after riding in cable cars and seeing some parts of La Paz from the birds' eye view, they take a stroll on famous Jaén Street and visit Plaza Murillo, the central plaza of La Paz.

"This place reminds me of the plazas we saw in Santiago and Lima. Look, this is a cathedral, a monument, and this looks like a government building. I am noticing that the main squares of big cities in South America look very similar," concludes Nick observing everything around him.

"Mom, I am hungry. What does that lady have?" asks Aya looking in the direction of a woman selling typical Bolivian foods and drinks.

They all eat ANTICUCHOS, a type of beef skewers with spices and potatoes, and API DE MAÍZ MORADO, a bright drink made of purple corn, orange zest and spices.

The following day the family rents a car and then drives for 4 hours to Oruro, situated southeast of La Paz.

"Mom, is Oruro the city where the carnival takes place? Can we attend it?" asks Nick.

"Yes. Carnival of Oruro is a big cultural event in Bolivia, where more than 40 groups of folk dancers perform a pilgrimage to a special place in a traditional parade," responds Kate.

In Oruro they go to the carnival and are impressed by the performance and bright colors on the streets.

"Can I wear a colorful costume, too?" wonders Aya.

In the afternoon her wish comes true. One of the dancers notices Aya wearing a carnival dress and invites the girl to dance in the parade.

The next day Nick is looking out the car window at ALTIPLANO, the beautiful landscape of high plains. All of a sudden he sees multiple pink spots on the horizon and says to his sister, "Aya, look at those birds! Do you remember seeing flamingoes for the first time in Argentine Patagonia?"

Aya excitedly moves closer to her brother. "Of course, I remember! There are a lot more of them here! I wish I could hold a baby flamingo! Look, Nick! Are those GUANACOS like the ones we saw in Argentina?" Aya points at the few animals crossing the road as their father slows down.

"These animals are called VICUÑAS," explains George. "Just like GUANACOS, VICUÑAS are wild relatives of llamas.

Soon they reach Uyuni, a town in the southwest of Bolivia known for the surrounding area of salt flats which is called SALAR in Spanish.

The next morning the adventurers move on to see the largest SALAR in the world.

"Dad, this place reminds me of the salt flats we saw in the Atacama Desert in Chile. This one looks so much bigger, though. I can't even see its end!" exclaims Nick.

"The area of Salar de Uyuni is over 10,000 square kilometers (3,900 square miles) and the layer of salt is a few meters deep," George tells him.

"Was it always like this?" asks Aya.

"Many thousands of years ago there were lakes. It is believed that now there are over 10 billion tons of salt here," answers her dad.

"I can't really imagine what this number means! But it sure is a unique place," adds Nick.

"Now that we feel adapted to high altitudes, we are ready for Potosí, another place of interest which is located at even higher elevation than La Paz, where we landed," shares Kate.

Upon arrival in Potosí, the kids get hungry. They all go to MERCADO CENTRAL or central market and buy SALTEÑAS which are little pies filled with different meats, olives, raisins and sometimes vegetables. Nick chooses the ones with chicken and Aya prefers a vegetarian kind. The kids drink MOCOCHINCHI, a cold, peach drink made with a little sugar and cinnamon.

They then go to CERRO RICO, the 'rich mountain' that brought a lot of silver to the Spanish Empire and made Potosí large and famous throughout the world at that time.

"This place doesn't look 'rich' to me at all!" declares Nick. "I thought it was going to have a palace here, instead these buildings look dirty, dusty and mostly ruined!"

"See that small door? This is the entrance to the inner part of the mountain. There is a narrow tunnel inside that was built by the workers. The further and deeper you go, the darker and stuffier it gets. It's called a mine. Mines are created to take away natural resources such as ore, copper, gold and in this case here, silver. Then the metal is taken to different factories and eventually is sold. Working conditions are very difficult, and often unsafe," George explains.

From Potosí, they continue on to another town called Sucre. Sucre is Bolivia's true capital. It is also called The White City because it has multiple white buildings created many years ago during the times of the Spanish Empire.

"Kids! Today we are going to see something really exciting - real dinosaur footprints!" Kate announces.

At the Cretacico Park they stand next to the Cal Orck'o cliff and stare in awe at the multiple footprints. Finally, Nick asks, "How many different dinosaurs do you think walked here?"

"Well, according to the official information there are footprints from about 15 species. Each footprint is up to 80 cm (32 inches) and there are over 5,000 of them," George responds.

Aya is puzzled. "I don't understand how they walked on this wall?"

"Well, some millions of years ago this wall wasn't a wall. It was a flat beach made of clay. The scientists discovered that a baby Tyrannosaurus Rex walked here and left a 347 meter (1,100 foot) long trail," Kate tells them.

George knows that his kids would like to step inside the dinosaur tracks. He takes the family to the Toro Toro National Park. Aya and Nick find 50-centimeters-long footprints which they study closely as they place their small feet inside the ancient giant steps.

After a walk through the area, they see Toro Toro Canyon.

"This place looks like a smaller version of the Grand Canyon back in the States!" declares Nick.

"What is that bird flying above the canyon, Mom?" wonders Aya. "It looks huge!"

"This looks like an Andean condor. Its wingspan can reach about 10 meters or 32 feet. It is a very large bird indeed!" Kate confirms.

"Dad, when and where are we going next for your work?" asks Nick.

"First we will have to drive for some time to the Isiboro Sécure Indigenous Territory and National Park and then, towards the end of our trip, to Madidi National Park," responds George.

After passing a city of Cochabamba, the travelers reach their new destination which looks lush and feels humid.

"Welcome to the Bolivian jungle!" declares Kate. "This national park is home to various tribes, diverse flora and fauna and multiple rivers that are part of the Amazon basin."

"What are we going to do here?!" Aya is curious.

"I have to observe the effects of deforestation on the local flora and record my findings. While I do that, you can go on a hike in the jungle. Once we are all done, we could go fishing all together," suggests George to everyone.

While their father is busy with his work, Aya and Nick discover the world of the Bolivian jungle with their mother. During the walk, they see a giant armadillo and a giant anteater.

Just like George suggested, they end their stay at this national park with fly fishing for Golden Dorado. This is Aya's first fly fishing experience outside of the United States and she is very excited to catch a fish that doesn't exist in her country.

After Isiboro Sécure National Park the family visits Madidi National Park in the northwestern part of Bolivia which occupies about 19,000 square kilometers (7,300 square miles). It is one of the largest protected areas on our planet.

They settle at one of the ecolodges located near the park entrance and begin a guided excursion to see the wildlife.

"Look around attentively. In this area we often meet a capybara. It is a giant rodent that is native to the South American continent and is considered the biggest in the world," says Juan, their guide.

While he is finishing his sentence both children notice a creature that resembles a bear.

"Is that a bear?" they both ask at the same time.

"Very good guess! This animal is called a spectacled bear. Let's stay here and observe it from the distance. We don't want to bother him," suggests George to his family. Later they see a capybara as well.

On their walk back to the lodge, Nick asks Juan about other languages he speaks.

"I also speak Spanish, but my native language is QUECHUA," responds the guide. "It is spoken in some parts of Bolivia, Peru, Ecuador, Colombia and Argentina."

"I want to learn some words in Quechua!" exclaims Aya.

"You already know one word and that is your name. In Quechua, the word AYA means 'soul'," explains Juan.

After the Madidi National Park, the family arrives in Copacabana, a city located at the shore of the Lake Titicaca. They then get in the boat and two hours later step on to ISLA DEL SOL or Island of the Sun in English.

"I remember from our trip to Peru that Lake Titicaca is the largest lake in South America," comments Nick.

"That is right, son!" exclaims his father as they approach a famous area of the island that has a sacred rock, ROCA SAGRADA.

"Why is this rock sacred?" asks Aya.

"According to one of the legends the first Inca state began here and the offerings to the Incan sun god named Inti were performed close to that labyrinth you can see over there," responds George while pointing at the ruins.

The kids first walk around the rocks of the labyrinth called LA CHINCANA and then play with local children and their llamas.

Nick, Aya and their parents Kate and George end their journey through Bolivia when they arrive back in La Paz and board a plane to fly home to the United States.

"You know, I really like meeting all these cool animals on our adventures," shares Aya with her brother.

"And I really like to look at things and places in different parts of the world," concludes Nick.

This book is dedicated to my daughter Aya who started traveling the world when she was 6 weeks old, and to my husband Justin who makes these travels possible.

Lightning Source UK Ltd.
Milton Keynes UK
UKHW020645011222
413095UK00002B/43